The *Zen* of Gardening

Wisdom Rooted in the Earth

LAINE CUNNINGHAM

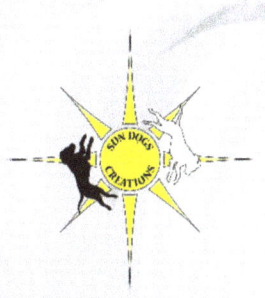

The Zen of Gardening:
Wisdom Rooted in the Earth

Published by Sun Dogs Creations
Changing the World One Book at a Time
Hardcover ISBN: 9780998224077
Softcover ISBN: 9780998224060

Cover Design by Angel Leya

Copyright © 2017 and 2019 Laine Cunningham

All rights reserved. No part of this book may be reproduced in any form or by any means, electronic, mechanical, digital, photocopying or recording, except for the inclusion in a review, without permission in writing from the publisher.

PRAISE FOR LAINE'S WORK

"Laine Cunningham combines tenacity and courage along with profound insight. Her bravery is contagious. I keep Laine's books on a special shelf in my library, referring to them when I need inspiration."

-Pamela King Cable, Author,
The Sanctum and *Televenge*

"The fact that Laine Cunningham spent six long months on her own in the Australian outback before writing this book leant a rich authenticity to her voice as she shared from her abundantly full, and talented, heart."

-Leah Griffith, Author, *Cosette's Tribe*

"Laine Cunningham ... is our spiritual messenger bringing us universal truths from an ancient yet extant culture. Mesmerizing and meaningful and inspiring."

-Grady Harp, Vine Voice,
Hall of Fame Reviewer

"Her goal is to assist each individual in identifying the message that is meaningful to them on their own individual journey. She defines a divine consciousness that has always resided within us personally ... Her concluding paragraph is an affirmation of life."

-Shirley, Goodreads Reviewer

"Laine Cunningham pulls you in, wraps you in a cocoon and pulls you through an enchanting, wonderful tale."

-A. Boxley, Goodreads Reviewer

INTRODUCTION

A few years ago, a tree I had nurtured through straight-line winds and hurricanes shattered. That night the weather was calm but a heavy rain had drenched the leaves. With the crackle of lightning, a large portion of the tree sheared off. A few minutes later, another section fell, sealing the tree's demise.

A garden took its place. That patch of new growth inspired additional gardens that border the property and the house. Roughly half the lawn has been replaced with flowers, blooming shrubs, and native trees.

This fall, a dump truck delivered enough mulch to refresh all those areas. As I shoveled...and shoveled...and shoveled through freezing temperatures and biting wind, the pile shrank. Like most challenges, six cubic yards of mulch disappears one shovelful at a time.

Thus was born *The Zen of Gardening.*

A WATER FEATURE
SOOTHES THE TUMBLING MIND.

A GARDEN'S BOUNTY NOURISHES THE ONE WHO GIVES OF ITS GIFTS.

REPELLING BEETLES AND GRUBS PRESERVES BEAUTY.

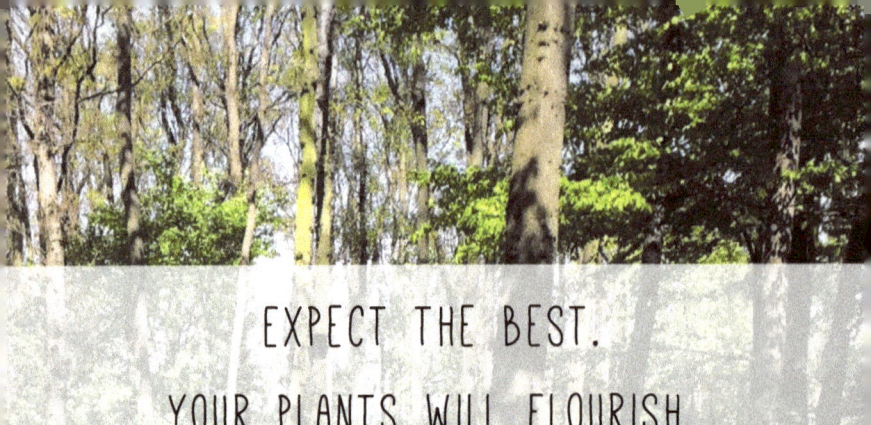

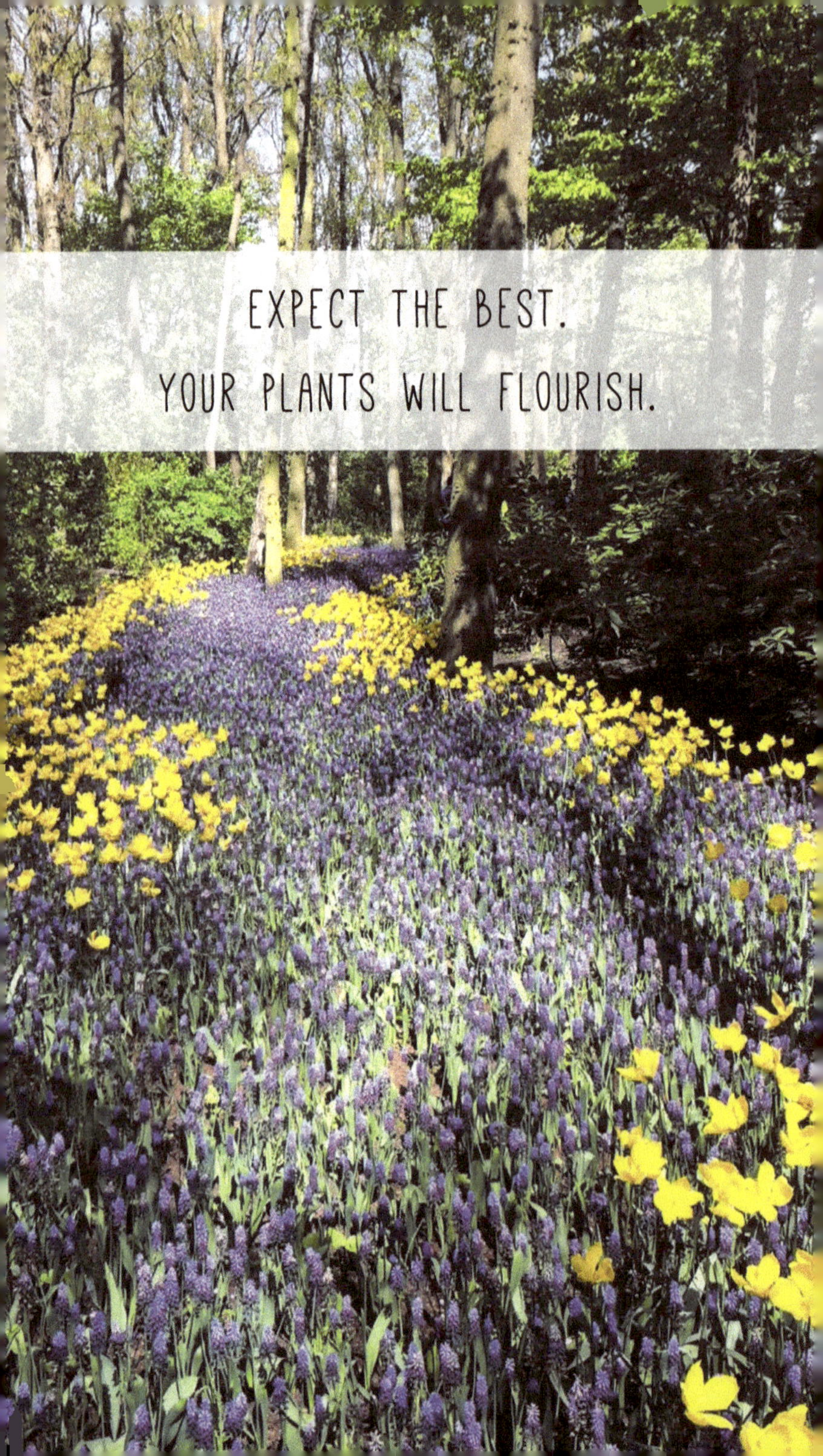
EXPECT THE BEST.
YOUR PLANTS WILL FLOURISH.

GRACE IS FOUND IN GRATITUDE
FOR ABUNDANT CROPS AND BLOOMS.

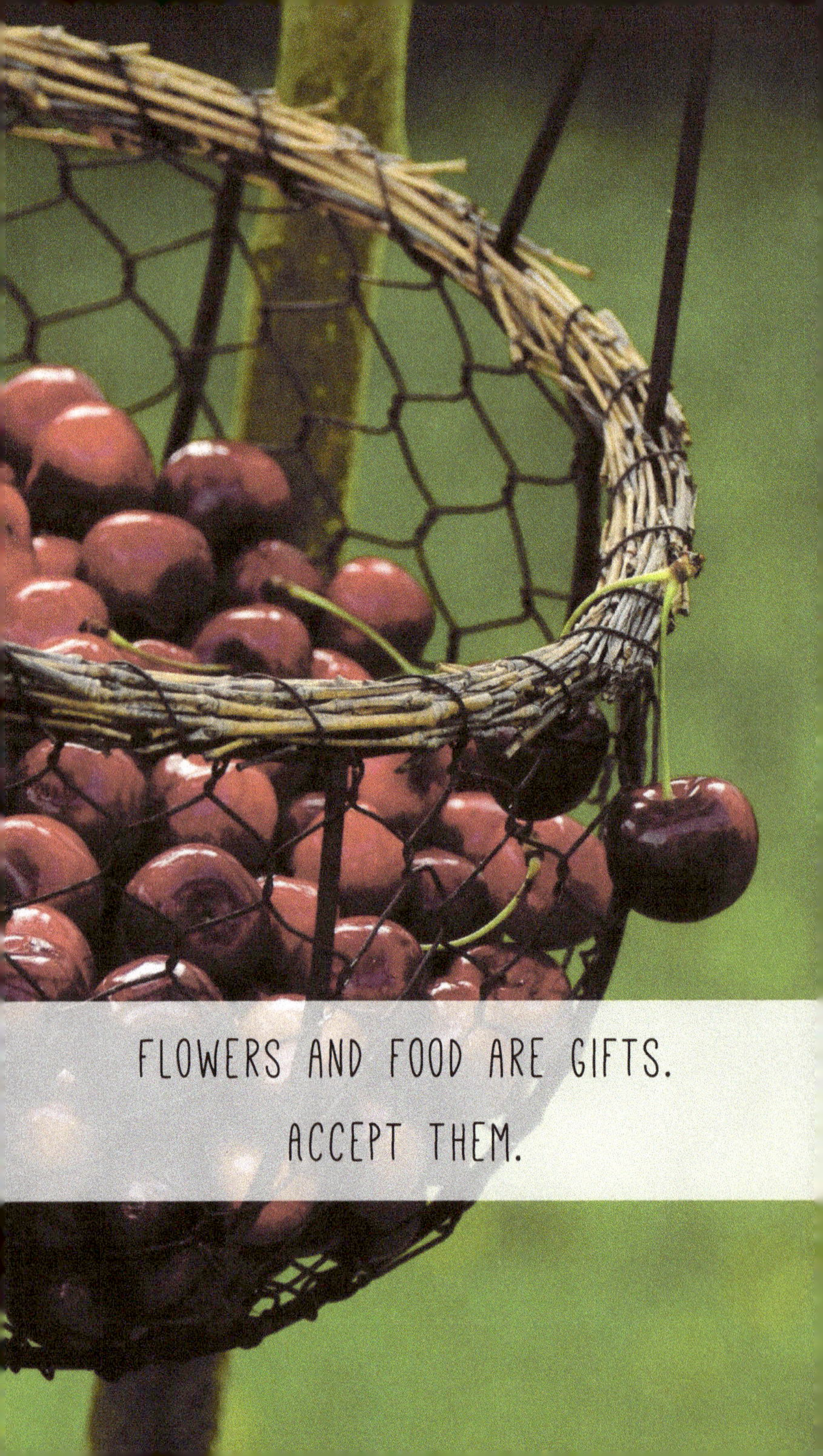

FLOWERS AND FOOD ARE GIFTS.

ACCEPT THEM.

CREATE A BEAUTIFUL SPACE
FOR YOUR NEIGHBORS AND YOURSELF.

CONSTANT VIGILANCE PREVENTS INFESTATION.

EVERY GARDEN

NEEDS A GNOME.

PLANT WISELY.
YOU REAP WHAT YOU SOW.

SUBDIVIDING CREATES SPACE FOR ALL THAT YOU LOVE.

LISTEN TO THE BREEZE
AND THE FALL OF AUTUMN LEAVES.

DIGGING DEEP
WELCOMES NEW PLANTS.

WATCHING THE WEATHER PREPARES AGAINST STORMS.

DEADHEADING SPENT BLOSSOMS
ENCOURAGES NEW GROWTH.

TRANSPLANTING BLESSES THE WORLD WITH YOUR BLOSSOMS.

COMPOSTING TURNS WASTE INTO A RICH RESOURCE.

RANGY PLANTS

ARE REACHING FOR MORE.

MULCH ENOUGH TO NURTURE
BUT NOT SO MUCH AS TO SMOTHER.

MODERATING YOUR METHODS PROVIDES FOR EVERY PLANT.

A SINGLE BENCH
BECOMES YOUR REFUGE.

BEES PACK A STING
TO PROTECT A GLISTENING TREASURE.

SELF-SEEDING ANNUALS ARE A TYPE OF PERENNIAL.

A BIRDFEEDER COMPLETES YOUR PARADISE.

PRUNING
IS REGENERATIVE.

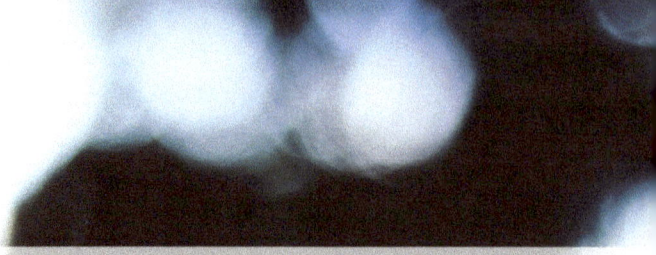

GROUND COVER PLANTED THOUGHTLESSLY BECOMES AN INVASIVE WEED.

A TROWEL, GIVEN DILIGENCE AND TIME, CAN MOVE A MOUNTAIN.

FEMALE TREES ARE MESSY
ONLY IN THE OVERLY FORMAL GARDEN.

PUSHING A WHEELBARROW IS AN EXERCISE IN BALANCE.

CENTIPEDE GRASS
MUST BE RIPPED OUT BY THE ROOTS.

GETTING DIRTY
IS A SIGN OF ENGAGEMENT.

THE MAGNIFICENT MONARCH WAS ONCE A VORACIOUS GRUB.

FLOWERS THAT OPEN AT NIGHT
ADD A MYSTICAL TOUCH.

SEEDS STORED FOR TOO LONG
LOSE THEIR VITALITY.

SQUIRRELS WILL SOW FOR YOU
IF YOU ARE OPEN TO SURPRISES.

REJOICE IN THE BEAUTY
YOU CREATE.

ABOUT THE AUTHOR

Laine Cunningham's books take readers on adventures around the world. *The Family Made of Dust* is set in the Australian Outback, while *Reparation* is a novel of the American Great Plains. Her women's travel adventure memoir *Woman Alone: A Six-Month Journey Through the Australian Outback* appeals to fans of *Wild* and *Eat Pray Love*. Her work has received multiple awards including the Hackney and the James Jones Fellowship, and has been published by *Reed, Birmingham Arts Journal*, and the annual anthology by *Writer's Digest*. She is the senior editor of *Sunspot Literary Journal*.

Fiction

The Family Made of Dust
Beloved
Reparation

Nonfiction

Woman Alone
On the Wallaby Track: Australian Words and Phrases
Seven Sisters: Messages from Aboriginal Australia
Writing While Female or Black or Gay
The Wisdom of Puppies
The Wisdom of Babies
The Wisdom of Weddings

The Zen of Travel
The Zen of Gardening
Zen in the Stable
The Zen of Chocolate
The Zen of Dogs

Bikes of Berlin
Necropolises of New Orleans I & II
Ruins of Rome I & II
Ancients of Assisi I & II
Panoramas of Portugal
Nuances of New York
Glimpses of Germany
Impressions of Italy
Altitudes of the Alps
Knights Through the Ages
Utopia of the Unicorn
Portraits of Paris
Flourishes of France

www.ingramcontent.com/pod-product-compliance
Lightning Source LLC
Chambersburg PA
CBHW040331300426
44113CB00020B/2718